WETLANDS

A Buddy Book
by
Fran Howard

ABDO
Publishing Company

VISIT US AT

www.abdopublishing.com

Published by ABDO Publishing Company, 4940 Viking Drive, Edina, Minnesota 55435.

Printed in the United States.

Edited by: Sarah Tieck
Contributing Editor: Michael P. Goecke
Graphic Design: Brady Wise
Image Research: Deb Coldiron, Maria Hosley, Heather Sagisser, Brady Wise
Photographs: Minden Pictures, Photodisc, photos.com, Superstock

Library of Congress Cataloging-in-Publication Data

Howard, Fran, 1953-
Wetlands / Fran Howard.
p. cm. — (Habitats)
Includes bibliographical references and index.
ISBN 1-59679-783-5 (10 digit ISBN)
ISBN 978-1-59679-783-3 (13 digit ISBN)
1. Wetlands—Juvenile literature. I. Title. II. Series: Habitats (Edina, Minn.)

QH87.3.H69 2006
577.68—dc22

2005032240

Table Of Contents

What Are Wetlands?

A view of a marsh.

Wetlands are low areas that flood with water. Bogs, marshes, and swamps are all wetlands.

Wetlands can be filled by rain. **Groundwater** that breaks through the soil can also fill a wetland. Flooded rivers and lakes form wetlands, too.

Canada has almost one-fourth of the world's wetlands.

Wetlands are one kind of habitat. Habitats are the places where plants and animals find food, water, and places to live. Different plants and animals live in different habitats. Many plants and animals live in wetlands.

Birds, such as Canadian geese, often live in wetlands.

Blueberries are one type of plant that grows in bogs. This bog is in Maine.

Where Are Wetlands Found?

Some wetlands have salt water and some have freshwater.

Wetlands are found all over the world. Bogs, marshes, and swamps are different kinds of wetlands.

Bogs are wet, muddy places where lakes used to be. Bogs are found in areas where it is cold, such as Canada. They are also found in tropical areas such as Africa and South America.

A white cedar bog in Minnesota.

Marshes are shallow. They can be found in warm or cold places. They are often found close to lakes and streams.

Swamps are found in warm areas. They are often found near coasts. Swamps have standing water. Sometimes, the water levels change.

A marsh

A swamp

WETLAND PLANTS

Plants that live in wetlands need a lot of water. Moss and peat are found in bogs. Peat is a soil made up of rotting plants. Walking on peat is like walking on a sponge.

Some trees grow in bogs, such as the black spruce. Plants that eat insects also grow in bogs.

A view of a peat bog. Some people use peat from bogs for fuel.

Sundew plants eat insects and live in bogs.

Cattails and grasses grow in marshes. But, very few trees or shrubs grow there.

In swamps, trees and shrubs are common. The bald cypress tree grows in swamps. Moss often hangs from the swamp trees. Water lilies are plants that grow in some swamps.

Cattails

Marsh grasses can survive in standing water.

Bog Animals

A mosquito

Only certain animals can live in a bog habitat. Mosquitoes live in bogs. So do dragonflies. Dragonflies are insects that eat other insects. They hunt mosquitoes while they fly.

Northern bog lemmings are small **rodents**. They live underground in **burrows** with their family. Lemmings eat plants, snails, and slugs.

A snail

A moose walking through a wetland.

Moose are the largest animals that live in bogs. Moose eat all kinds of plants. They use trails made by other moose when walking through the bog. Moose have wide hooves to help them walk on the spongy soil in a bog.

Marsh Animals

Many animals live in marshes. Frogs live in marshes. Frogs have long, sticky tongues. They catch bugs with their tongues.

Frogs **hibernate** through the cold weather. They bury themselves in mud or sand. They can breathe through their skin. Frogs stay close to their marsh when they hibernate.

A frog

These turtles are in the water.

Turtles also live in marshes. Turtles spend most of the time in the water. They crawl onto rocks or logs to sit in the sun. Turtles have hard shells. When a turtle is in danger, it hides in its shell.

Red-winged blackbirds live in marshes, too. They make their nests in cattails. During the day, blackbirds form huge flocks to look for seeds. At night, they return to the marshes.

A red-winged blackbird

SWAMP ANIMALS

Many animals live in swamps. Snapping turtles are one kind of animal living in swamps. They spend most of their lives in the water.

Snapping turtles are active at night. They have strong jaws and webbed feet. Snapping turtles eat plants, fish, frogs, bugs, and other small **mammals**.

Water moccasins are poisonous swamp snakes. They are good climbers. They rest on branches that hang over the water.

A water moccasin

Many birds also live in swamps, such as the white ibis. The white ibis has a curved red bill. It eats bugs, frogs, snakes, and fish.

A white ibis

Alligators are large swamp animals. They spend most of their time in the water. Alligators are good swimmers. Their large tail and webbed feet help them swim.

Alligators hunt mostly at night. They eat fish, birds, turtles, and small land animals. Alligators swallow their **prey** whole.

An American alligator

Why Are Wetlands IMPORTANT?

People and animals need wetlands. Wetlands store water. This helps control flooding.

People use wetlands for hunting and fishing. They also use wetlands to study nature.

Over the years, people have drained wetlands. In the United States, half of the wetlands have been drained.

Many wetlands have been drained to grow crops.

Moose

Dragonfly

Mosquito

Plants and animals of wetlands cannot live without their habitat. And, they need each other to survive. Together they form a **food chain**. Even the smallest plants and animals are part of the food chain.

These African elephants depend on this wetland for survival.

WETLANDS

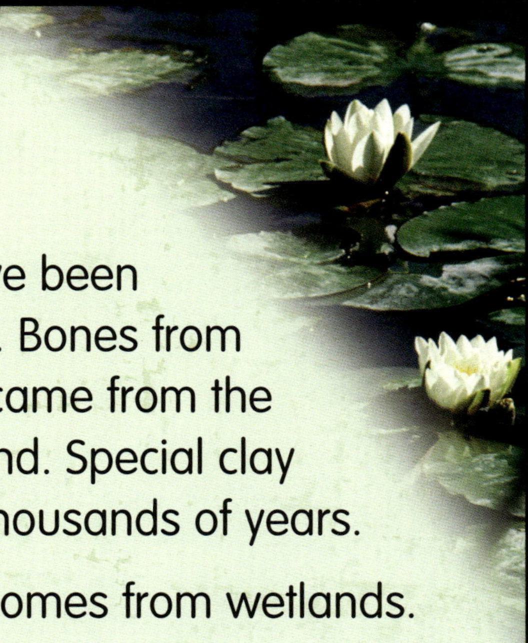

- Many animal fossils have been found in bogs in Ireland. Bones from more than 100 Irish elk came from the Ballybetagh Bog in Ireland. Special clay saved these bones for thousands of years.
- Wild rice is a food that comes from wetlands.
- There is another kind of wetland. It is called a fen. Fens are known for being rich in minerals. The soil is not the same as other wetlands. It is covered with moving water.
- There is a marshmallow plant that grows in saltwater marshes. People would use it to make medicine for colds and sore throats. This plant is not used to make the kind of marshmallows people put in hot cocoa.

Important Words

burrow a hole or a tunnel dug in the ground by an animal.

food chain the order in which plants and animals feed on each other.

groundwater water in the earth that supplies wells and springs.

hibernate to sleep during the winter months.

mammal most living things that belong to this special group have hair, give birth to live babies, and make milk to feed their babies.

prey an animal that is food for other animals.

rodent an animal with sharp front teeth for gnawing.

Web Sites

Would you like to learn more about **wetlands**? Please visit ABDO Publishing Company on the World Wide Web to find Web site links about **wetlands**. These links are routinely monitored and updated to provide the most current information available.

www.abdopublishing.com

INDEX